SHANNON ARONSON, MSW
REALTOR

DON'T GIVE IT AWAY

Maximize The Sales Price Of Your Home By
Discovering The Emotional Mistakes Every Home
Seller Makes... And How To Avoid Them

This book is dedicated to my beautiful family and friends, my loyal clients and my devoted team...
I am honored to serve and help you each day.

Shannon Aronson, MSW, Realtor^(R)

My clients, colleagues, friends
and family describe me as...

TABLE OF CONTENTS

trustworthy

INTRODUCTION

"I don't want to give it away," said the seller at our listing appointment. I understood her concern. But having heard that refrain countless times during my career as one of New Jersey's top producing realtors, I realized it was time to write this book. For many people, their home is their largest financial asset. For most, it also holds significant emotional attachment and the fear of "giving it away" for less than its maximum value cuts to the heart of some very deep-seated emotions and vulnerability for homeowners.

This book is designed to help clients understand the selling process, the underlying feelings involved, and how to avoid the costly mistakes many sellers make as a result of emotional rather than rational decision making.

Over the years, I have noticed while helping clients sell their homes, just how often they are also juggling multiple other life stressors, both positive and negative.

a leader

In addition to selling their home, they may be growing their family, sending a child to college, adjusting to an empty nest, relocating for work, going through a separation or divorce, or dealing with a sick or recently deceased loved one.

Sellers don't want to feel as though they are "giving their house away," and rightfully so. Selling a home on its own can be a stressful endeavor. Add on other major life transitions, and it can all seem like it's too much to handle.

This is when my master's degree in clinical social work and certification and training in psychotherapy are extremely useful. Because of my background, my team and I are uniquely able to help clients successfully navigate the home selling process.

experienced

As much as sellers don't want to feel that they are selling their home at a discount, we don't want them to feel that way either; the right listing price is vital for the success of the sale, and also for the peace of mind of the sellers.

Our job is to help clients maximize the value of their home and put the most money in their pockets.

This book contains advice I've shared with clients on how to feel more in control of the home selling process. We help them manage the extreme stress that goes along with selling a house during major life transitions, and come out on the other side with a successful sale.

This book will help educate you on how to avoid emotional and costly mistakes, show you what to expect during the sale process, and encourage you to put the right team in place to help minimize your stress during your home selling experience, while maximizing your profits.

To Your Success!

Shannon Aronson

professional

GETTING STARTED

Selling your home can be a daunting task, especially if you aren't familiar with the process. For every person ready to sell a home, there are many more who want to sell, or who would benefit from selling, but put it off, unsure where or how to begin. There are many reasons clients get stuck and become paralyzed before they even get started.

organized

If you are considering a move, you will likely have many questions, such as:

- Is it the right time to sell?

- What is the right list price?

- What is the process and how long will it take?

- Who are the right people to help get it sold?

- Do I need to redo the bathroom?

- Where will I put all the extra stuff I have stored in the basement?

You are not alone in asking these questions. I'm here to tell you that there are answers to all these questions, and any others that arise. My team and I can help you find them.

visionary

You don't have to be one of the many people I see daily that can't move forward with the sale of their home because they let these common roadblocks get in the way.

Common Issues That Often Get People Stuck:

- Feeling overwhelmed by the volume of "decluttering" that needs to be done.

- Being unsure of the optimal balance between spending money preparing the house for sale, and feeling confident that spending is a wise investment.

- Not having the money or the time to get the home in its best shape to sell, but dreading the thought of "giving it away" simply because one can't afford to get the home looking its best.

- Having different views from one's partner about moving, finances, the division of labor in preparing for the sale or choosing a realtor.

- Being unable to determine where they will move to, until they have a good understanding of what price they will get for their home, but not being willing to put their home on the market without knowing where they will go.

- Disagreeing over selling a marital home before a divorce agreement is finalized, particularly when the equity in the house will finance the ability to separate and lawyers advise waiting.

proactive

- Experiencing difficulty reconciling that a chapter in one's life is ending can lead people to hang on to a home that may no longer meet their needs, or that may over-tax their pocketbooks.

- Managing the sale of an estate when multiple decision makers are involved; getting all parties onboard emotionally and financially can keep a home's sale "stuck" for a long while.

- Having an emotional reaction to a change or loss, such as in the case of empty nesters, the recently widowed or divorced, can make the process of home selling difficult to begin.

My job is to help clients better understand how these roadblocks can impact the home selling process so they go into it with more confidence and less weighty baggage. Together, we identify what to expect along the way so clients can take control of the process and their own emotions.

Ultimately, this allows the home selling process to be less stressful AND more successful. In life, as in home selling, the expression "cooler heads prevail" is true. When the stress of the selling process is minimized, the best outcome is achieved.

This book will help sellers, like you, better understand the home selling process. This will enable you to list your home with confidence and minimal disruption to your life, and ultimately achieve top dollar for your home.

innovative

WHEN IS THE RIGHT TIME
TO SELL YOUR HOME?

This is usually one of the first questions clients ask as they explore selling their home. Should they wait for spring? Or perhaps winter is the right time to sell when inventory is lighter? Coupled with the common issue of not being entirely certain where they're going to live after they sell their home, the issue of timing can create a lot of angst, indecision and delays.

charismatic

The good news is that the answer is quite simple. The right time to sell your home is when it's the right time for you, given what's happening in your life. Most people sell their home for a reason. So, first you'll need to get very clear about the reasons for selling your home. Then, determine how that fits with where you need or want to go. That's more important than trying to time your sale based on the season or whether the market is up or down.

public speaker

Skeptical about this advice? Let me explain why it holds true. People typically think spring is the best time to sell a home because they feel the pool of potential homebuyers is greatest at that time. While that happens to be true in most years and in most markets, you need to consider that spring also has the most homes on the market. While the market may be flooded with buyers, it's usually equally flooded with sellers.

grateful

If you need or want to sell your home in the fall or winter based on important events in your life, keep in mind that there will still be buyers and likely fewer homes on the market competing with yours. So, your home may actually end up being more competitive given the scarcity of inventory during those months of the year.

purposeful

VALUING YOUR HOME
AND PRICING MYTHS

Selling at the right price is perhaps the prime concern for sellers. That's why it is important for my clients not only to have a clear sense of the value of their home, but also of the process for determining that value. Once you understand how the market values your home, you can avoid sleepless nights and feel confident that you're not giving it away.

Before I outline how to price your home, let's review how NOT to determine the price of your home. I call them the WENS Myths.

a big picture thinker

What are the WENS Myths?

The W stands for "Want."

Sellers usually say to me, "I really want X dollars for my home." Typically, that figure contains a lot of sentimental value. I have to advise them, "It's great that you *want* a certain price for your home, but what you want has nothing to do with the value of the home and what the market will actually determine that value to be. Unfortunately, buyers won't pay extra because your children took their first steps in the living room."

pragmatic

The E stands for "Ego Pricing."

Nearly every time I sit down with a seller, I hear something along the lines of "yeah, but I know my house is more desirable than the guy's two doors down, and he sold it for X dollars six months ago, and I definitely have a better backyard."

Clients are acutely aware of the best one or two features of their home because in most cases, it was the feature that caused them to fall in love with their home in the first place. Often, clients use their neighbor's selling price, pick one or two traits about their home that are better, and adjust their expectations upward accordingly.

They don't consider that every other house also has a best feature, and they often discount the less desirable features of their own home disproportionately. Interestingly, if they didn't happen to like their neighbor, they bump up the perceived value of their own home even more.

Their ego believes their house is better, so in turn, they want a better price. Ego pricing is clearly not an effective way to determine the price of your home.

strong

N stands for "Need."

At least once a week I hear a client say something like this, "I really need to get $550,000 for my home because the retirement community I'm going to will cost me that amount of money." Or, "I really need $1,000,000 for my home, because when I downsize, I need to put a little money away for my retirement."

Unfortunately, what you need to get out of your home and its market value have nothing to do with one another. There is absolutely zero correlation between the two.

independent

Lastly, the S stands for "Spent."

I'm sure most of you have thought to yourself, "Well, I bought the house for $600,000 and I spent another $100,000 on the house in upgrades, so I need to get back what I spent. Therefore, the house should be priced at $700,000 at the very least, plus closing costs."

Well, guess what? I hate to break it to you, but what you spent on upgrades or fixes to your kitchen, bathrooms or roof may or may not be reflected in the value of your home.

The fact that you spent a certain amount on the home and want to get that back, is certainly understandable. However, it has nothing to do with the actual value of your home.

dependable

SET YOUR LIST PRICE

Now that we've covered how NOT to value your home, we can put all that information aside and focus on the things that really will determine the price of your home.

In the simplest terms, your home is worth what someone is willing to pay for it on any given day.

People often think pricing their home for sale is an exact science. In practice, pricing a home is very far from an exact science.

A realtor, certified bank appraiser, neighbor, friend, mother-in-law, may all give you pricing advice. At the end of the day, they really offer only educated or, in some cases, uneducated opinions.

nonjudgemental

Please understand that the value of your home, at any given time, will fall within a large, variable price range. If you accept this, you are much more likely to minimize the stress associated with selling a home and achieve a speedy sale.

So how do you determine the right price range for your home?

Educate yourself about your local market. One of the first things you should do is compare your home to other homes in your area that have recently sold and those that are currently on the market.

You are likely to be biased when comparing your house to others. This is normal and very important to keep in mind.

serious

Your neighbors will also frequently suffer from this same inability to be objective about the current value of the neighborhood, so it is best to have a third party weigh in.

A realtor can prepare a report of comparable properties, and you can do some legwork of your own too. Take a look on the Internet or by driving around town to learn about the features those other homes have or don't have compared to yours.

- How many bedrooms do they have?

- How many bathrooms do they have?

- How big is their lot?

- Which neighborhood do you feel is more desirable?

- Are there any drawbacks to the homes you are comparing?

- What is the differential in the property tax assessments?

assertive

This process will allow you to get an objective sense of the other homes that you'll be competing against.

The second thing that you can do is look at relevant market data. Let's take the price band that you believe your home will most likely fall within, somewhere between $600,000 and $800,000, for example. Your next step is to find out how many homes sold in that price range in the past 12 months.

If, for example, there were 24 homes in that price band that sold during the past year, you'll know that, on average, 2 homes in your price band sell per month.

Why is this important?

respectful

It helps you price your home competitively. Here's how. If you look at the homes that are actively on the market, and you know that in the next month, most likely, only two of those will sell, you know that if you want your home to sell in the next month you will need to be one of the two best homes in that price band.

Your home will need to offer a better value than all of the other homes within that range to ensure that yours is one of the two that, according to data, will likely sell. Remember, best value isn't the same as least expensive. Your list price should account for the specific features of your home relative to others that are for sale, as well as the overall competitive landscape.

Now, many people wonder, should they have an appraiser come over or should they talk to different realtors for a market analysis? That's a very good question, and often times I recommend both. Realtors are on the front lines, taking buyers out on a daily basis, and they typically have a very good flavor for the other homes that are currently on the market - their attributes, what they're worth, how they will be viewed by buyers in comparison to yours.

unafraid

Typically, realtors do have a very good sense of what your home's market value is. Many people find they like to interview more than one realtor, while others find that a real estate agent's data combined with their own research can give them a thorough understanding of the market value.

I strongly advise that when you're talking to a real estate agent in order to determine the price of your home, you first determine which realtor you feel most comfortable with.

Once you establish a rapport with your chosen realtor, you can then review the market data and define a pricing strategy together. This is a much better approach than interviewing three realtors and deciding to hire the one that gave you the highest price estimate.

practical

Realtors often face a lot of pressure to come up with a high number just to make you happy and feed your ego. Ultimately, this may not be an accurate reflection of what your home is worth. Having inaccurate information and false hopes could lead you down an unpleasant emotional road that could be costly if you do list your home at too high a price.

Bank appraisers, by their nature, tend to look in the rear-view mirror when valuing property. They're looking at what has sold and closed during the past three to six months. While that is valuable information, it may not reflect what's happening in the market at the time you are selling your home.

intelligent

Nonetheless, it will give you a sense of where your home will appraise should your buyers need to obtain a mortgage to make the purchase. Remember, if the agreed upon selling price is significantly greater than the appraisal value and your buyers aren't paying cash for the home, they may not get the financing in order to close the deal. This could result in you relisting your home or renegotiating the price at the eleventh hour. In some cases, it may make sense to have both a realtor and a bank appraiser provide their assessments of your home's value.

honest

A final word of advice on setting your list price: don't be greedy. The old expression, "pigs get slaughtered," comes to mind and tends to be true when selling your home.

Data suggests that for every $10,000 over market value you price your home, in the end you'll likely lose about $6,000 of what you could have achieved for your home in the first place.

Why is this so? If you overprice your home, and it sits on the market for 30 days or 60 days or 90 days, it will be viewed as stale inventory, or having something wrong with it.

Buyers who see a home sitting on the market month after month may not even look at it, because they assume there must be something wrong with it, or that it will be difficult for them to resell when that day arrives.

progressive

They may believe that the sellers aren't realistic about the price of their home, and they don't want to buy a home that's sitting on the market, overpriced. This can lead buyers to believe that they have greater negotiating leverage over the price.

There's usually a pattern of mistakes when it comes to homes that are priced too high, and it looks something like this ... The first mistake: the home is listed at too high of a price. The second mistake: sellers wait way too long before reducing the price. The third mistake: desperation results in a poor negotiating position and sellers end up getting slaughtered.

a brilliant negotiator

By the time the sellers acknowledge what they actually want and need to sell their home, and that they are willing to reduce the price, it has been on the market for too long, has become stale, and has earned a reputation as an undesirable house. When the price is finally lowered, the home is worth less than it would have been if it had been priced correctly when it first went on the market.

This is where an experienced real estate agent can really help, but only if sellers are willing to put emotion aside and price their home according to market data. Advising clients where in the price band to list a home so that the house attracts maximum buyer interest is one of the most important reasons to hire a realtor.

Hiring the right real estate agent, and deciding to rely on his or her expertise, will minimize costly mistakes. This will save you time and money, and reduce the overall stress related to selling your home.

WHEN PRICING YOUR HOME, AVOID THE "WENS" MINDSET, DO YOUR HOMEWORK, WORK WITH PROFESSIONALS THAT MIGHT BE MORE OBJECTIVE ABOUT YOUR HOME THAN YOU ARE, AND DON'T BE GREEDY.

reasonable

RE-EVALUATE YOUR
PRICING STRATEGY

Sometimes you need to re-evaluate your pricing strategy. Keep in mind that the WENS Myths - the Wants, your Ego, what you Need, and what you Spent - should NOT be revisited weekly while your home is on the market. These myths are not an effective pricing tool, but sellers frequently fall back on them, especially when the home isn't selling quickly.

Instead, focus on the market. Talk to your real estate agent to determine what has changed since you first listed your property. Are there more properties available for sale? Did the mortgage rates go up? What homes sold in the same price range while your home did not? Should you stage your home if you haven't previously? What feedback do you have from prospective buyers? All of these factors may impact if, when, and by how much, you alter your list price. Most importantly, let the data, not your emotions, drive your pricing strategy.

a quick thinker

MAINTAIN YOUR SANITY
WHILE SELLING

Before I was a real estate agent, I was a psychotherapist. I have a master's degree in social work and additional training in psychotherapy. I have found that helping people sell a home is a lot like short-term psychotherapy.

Let's face it, selling a home is stressful. There are a lot of triggers that make people agitated throughout the home selling process. Sometimes, sellers can feel as though they are losing a bit of their sanity. To help stay sane while selling your home, it is helpful to understand what to expect. This allows you to put your reactions and emotions in perspective, feel a bit more normal, and much less susceptible to stress.

There are also special challenges to consider in keeping your sanity when you are making decisions as part of a couple. Whether you are married or not, everyone knows that financial matters can often be a source of tremendous stress for couples. Recently, a client of mine confided to me that she was "born with a beautiful silver spoon in her mouth," but her now very financially successful husband was not. This resulted in emotional arguments over things as mundane as the overuse of ziplock bags in their multi-million dollar vacation home.

fair

This client understood her own and her husband's emotional triggers. The very emotionally charged nature of selling a home, different levels of risk aversion between each partner, differences in motivation over selling and/or moving in the first place, and differences in how people feel about change, can make the home selling process a powder keg waiting to explode for couples who are usually not in complete lockstep over all of these factors.

My best advice to keep a relationship intact while selling a home is to understand and normalize the rather extreme feelings you are likely to experience towards your partner during this process. You may look at your partner or spouse with utter disdain at many moments throughout the process. That is normal. But, remember to remain focused on your goal – to sell your home for the best possible price in the shortest amount of time. The following are just a few examples, which I experience on a regular basis, of how the home selling process can lead to temporary couple turmoil.

faithful

- You may feel that your otherwise smart, savvy husband seems like he is ready to "give your house away," when he eagerly wants to accept that seemingly "low-ball offer" from the "bottom feeding" potential buyer.

- You may think your generally pragmatic, financially conservative wife has lost her mind when she insists that you can't list your current home for sale until you have a new home under contract. You'll find yourself wondering "how can she possibly think we can handle two mortgages without going bankrupt?"

- A well-respected, highly polished, usually peace-loving female colleague once told me that she wanted to "throw her husband against the wall" when he wouldn't accept an offer on their home because he refused to take his ego out of the equation and accept that the offer reflected what their house was worth.

- An extremely successful client who worked as a Wall Street executive, who was 37 weeks pregnant with her third child under the age of five, and had her entire house already packed in the moving truck, walked away from a closing while arguing with the potential buyers over a $200 issue discovered during the walk through. Her husband eventually talked her off of the ledge and back into the closing conference room, but it was pretty ugly for a few hours while she was essentially homeless.

ethical

This was a multi-million dollar transaction, so the $200 was a very small amount to pay to get the closing over with and get her family moving into their new home. It was a classic case of emotions getting in the way and potentially causing a very expensive debacle. They are currently living happily in their beautiful new home. But, as you can imagine, the stress on their marriage for a few hours was extreme.

What should you do if you think your partner has completely lost his or her mind in the midst of selling your home? First, remind yourself that this is probably normal and that you stand a very good chance of liking him or her again when the process is all over. Second, understand that the emotions involved in selling a home are very deep-seated and can make an issue that would normally be minor, become irrationally over-charged. If possible, when things become emotionally charged, wait a while, even "sleep on it" if that's possible, then try to start a conversation by acknowledging your partner's feelings about whatever issue is at hand. Try to find an element of their position that makes sense to you on any level and start by verbally validating it. Next, ask yourself if your partner is acting in a way that she or he feels is protecting the safety and best interest of your family.

Even if you believe his or her actions and thoughts are misguided, the intent is typically to protect loved ones. If that is true, let him or her know you see, feel, and appreciate that. Then, calmly try reminding your partner that often emotions can get in the way of making sound financial decisions when selling a home. Lastly, if you have put together a team of professionals that you trust to help you through the process, rely on those professionals to do the heavy lifting of getting your partner to use logic rather than emotions to get through the home sale process successfully.

an expert

GET OVER IT, YOU'LL
LOSE YOUR PRIVACY

One of the biggest issues for sellers is that once a property is listed for sale, their once private home enters the public domain. When a home is on the market, it's a commodity. It's no longer a home, but rather a property. People are going to be in and out of the home at all times, whether or not it's convenient for the sellers. Often, strangers in the form of home stagers or contractors come in before you even put your home on the market and give you advice about doing all sorts of things to your home that you may feel make it a whole lot less homey and a whole lot less yours. This is the first step in distancing yourself emotionally from your home. You have to accept that your home is going to essentially become public property.

After that process is complete and there is a sign in your front yard, buyers expect that they can come and go from your home at their pleasure. Let's think about an open house. A lot of times, clients will say to me, "I don't want to have an open house for my home. There's just going to be a bunch of nosy neighbors." That is actually true. You may have a lot of nosy neighbors parading through your home even though you'll feel they have no business being there.

generous

But, the truth is your nosy neighbors might have friends that are of like mind and of like socioeconomic status that may be your perfect buyers.

You can't sell a secret. You need to let your home become public property so everyone and anyone who's out there looking for a home is exposed to it and knows about it. This will increase the likelihood of them coming into your home and increase the odds of you selling it.

There is something else to consider as your home becomes public property. It shifts from being your home to being more like an aspirational furniture showroom. When people come in your home, they want to envision themselves in the home, not wonder who the people in the pictures are. You also don't want them trying to determine the religious or ethnic background of the sellers. This becomes a distraction. You'd rather have them thinking about the beautiful room proportions and how their furniture will fit into the space.

For example, you might have someone who's a diehard Republican looking at a house where they see a picture of someone standing next to their favorite Democratic past president.

calm

Although that may seem like it's not going to make much of a difference to most people, you'll want to get rid of all the things that could be negative triggers for buyers that may prevent or get in the way of them seeing themselves in your home. In addition, we want to dissuade buyers from making certain assumptions about the sellers that would affect the offer and subsequent negotiations.

A few pointers to keep in mind:

- Put away 90 percent of your personal pictures.

- Remove as many religious symbols as you are comfortable with.

- Put away items that are overly nationalistic. We typically recommend storing flags rather than displaying them.

This may strike you as harsh, but you should think of your home as no more than a furniture showroom.

> YOU HAVE TO ACCEPT THAT YOUR HOME WILL BE IN THE PUBLIC DOMAIN. YOU CAN'T SELL A SECRET.

accomplished

If you were to walk into a local Ethan Allen furniture store, you'd simply see furniture and possibly one or two strategically placed accessories, and that's it.

Often, this makes sellers feel uncomfortable. Their home no longer feels like their home. This is really the first step in letting go of your home and moving on. Given the fact that you're going to be moving on to a new property anyway, this is really the right time to begin that process. Think of it as another step, albeit a big step, in the journey towards letting go of your home and moving on to your next phase in life.

focused

Protecting personal property during the sales process is something a lot of people worry about.

Whether they are sentimental items or hold monetary value, people worry that once their home becomes public property and people are walking in and out, their valuables may be at risk.

This is a legitimate concern. Fortunately, there are ways to mitigate this risk:

- Remove anything that is of high value from the house.

- Small valuables that could be easily picked up and placed in a pocket should be put out of sight or even in a safety-deposit box.

Remember, private showings are conducted by a real estate professional who must enter a unique code to access the property. Buyers don't enter the home alone and there is a record of who entered and when they entered.

principled

A newer issue that I have experienced is medicine cabinet privacy and theft. If you have prescription medications that are easily accessible, please consider moving them to a secure, private location. This is more likely to be an issue at a public open house rather than a private showing of your home with a trained and seasoned realtor.

Nonetheless, for your own privacy and safety, take a moment to look at your bathroom and your medicine cabinets with an eye towards putting away any medications that might be tempting for someone to take.

confident

MANAGE LIFE STRESSES WHILE SELLING

Now that you've accepted that you'll lose your privacy, let's address some of the other things that may cause you anxiety during the process. Because I am a former psychotherapist, my ears perk up a little bit more than other realtors' about how stressful this whole process really is. Most people move for a reason. Usually, that reason involves a major life transition. Perhaps they are getting married, having a baby, or getting divorced. Perhaps there's been a death in the family. Perhaps a new job, decreasing income, or job loss is motivating the move. Or, maybe they're moving to a new community, having health issues, or downsizing out of a home that they may have lived in for forty years.

In addition to the stressful nature of selling your home, the reason for selling may be stressful as well. What this means is that most of the time, sellers are dealing with two major life stressors at the same time. Often, very intelligent, sane, calm, high-functioning people are burdened by these stressors. It becomes difficult for them to think clearly and make smart, unemotional decisions about the sale of their home, which may be a significant part of their financial portfolio.

determined

Often, people decompensate somewhat emotionally due to all this stress, which simply makes the whole process so much worse. I've seen people make foolish decisions about the sale of their home because of all this stress.

A friend once confided that after the fourth or fifth crisis involving mortgage and inspection issues during the sale of his house, he literally ran and hid in his car in his driveway, and told his wife simply to "deal with it." This is a high-functioning individual who handles a lot of stress as a partner in a successful law firm. He simply couldn't handle one more stressor at that point in time. When you're starting the home sale process, you need to sit down and understand how many stressors and how many transitions you're currently going through. You also need to acknowledge that this is going to be a difficult time for you.

Know who you can count on to help you through this process. Understand that it's going to be normal if you think you're flipping out. Understand that anger is often one of the major things that people feel when they're under this much stress, and that anger might be directed at the people that you love who live in this home with you. It might be directed at the realtor who you're feeling isn't doing his or her job. It may very well be directed at the buyer who you worry is stealing your home from you.

fun

Often, it's just anger about the entire process and how much control you feel you've lost in making your home a public commodity, and concern that you won't be extracting full value from it.

And, if you're moving out of one house, you're most likely moving into another. The vast majority of people are not only going through all this stress on the sale side, but also going through it on the buy side. You may feel that you are not getting enough money on the sale of your home, and undoubtedly you feel you're overpaying on the purchase of your new home.

Rest assured. You're not alone in feeling this way. Nonetheless, this absolutely adds a tremendous amount of anger, stress and angst to the entire process. Anticipate these feelings. Be ready for them.

Embrace them. Establish coping strategies and support systems so you can deal with your emotions without letting them sabotage your transaction.

loyal

So, what can you do to help prepare yourself to cope with the stresses as they arise?

1. Normalize the Process. Just the fact that you are reading a book about how your emotions can lead you to make costly mistakes is a step in the right direction. Prepare yourself to be upset and then tell yourself, "oh yes, I was told this is normal." Whatever range of feelings you experience is most likely normal, and just remembering that can often help you minimize the likelihood of taking irrational actions or making bad decisions in the heat of emotion.

kind

2. If you share the decision-making with someone else, it is best to have a conversation in advance about how you will handle emotionally charged situations. Here are a few tips about what to cover in that conversation:

- You would be well served to acknowledge verbally that it is normal for the process to be contentious, even when you are on the same side and you both agree to refrain from making decisions in moments of anger or elevated emotions.

- I recommend that you have a good understanding of what your priorities are, and a well-articulated understanding of what you hope to gain by selling your home. It will be easier to endure the bumps if you keep clear sight of the positive reasons that you are undertaking this in the first place.

- Take some time to gain insight as to what issues typically throw you into a tailspin: money, uncertainty, fear of change, feeling taken advantage of, or having to endure perceived insults about your home. These are all topics that have varying degrees of importance to different people. If you receive negative feedback about your home and subsequently feel depressed and angry for two days, it is best to not let those feelings interfere with the negotiation process. Own up to your own emotional "hotspots."

empathetic

3. Tell your most trusted friend or confidant that you may need a little extra ear-bending time over the next few months. Having someone available to "talk you off the ledge" will come in handy.

level-headed

4. If you really feel the stress of the situation is reaching a fever pitch, be kind to yourself and seek out some professional guidance. Trust me when I tell you I have seen people suffer unexpected and serious health issues when stressed over the issues we are discussing. Emotions can get out of hand when selling a home and dealing with other life stressors as well. Don't take this lightly... your health is more important than any real estate or financial transaction.

insightful

5. Help protect the mental health of the others involved as well. If you have children, ask them often about their thoughts about the move. Use open-ended questions such as "what do you think about the move and how it is going?" or "what do you think are the best and worst things about selling our house?" Children have even less control over the situation than we do as adults, and they may be struggling with issues that you haven't even thought about. Don't assume the worst, just keep an open ear. This may be a challenge if your child has made their displeasure about the move known. In that case you may feel the urge not to ask, as you know you cannot make their disappointment go away. It is still better to show a willingness to hear what is good and bad about the move for them, and be willing to hear their disappointment without overreacting. If their level of emotional upset seems worrying to you, it may be beneficial to consult a mental health professional to help deal with the difficult transition.

One of the most important ways you can create the professional and emotional support structure you need is by hiring the right team to help you with the sale of your home.

> MOST OF THE TIME, SELLERS ARE DEALING WITH TWO MAJOR LIFE STRESSORS AT THE SAME TIME.

motivated

HIRE THE RIGHT HOME SELLING TEAM

You're the boss. It's your home and you are in control of the decisions related to your home. Being informed is a key part of making the right decisions. And, in order to make smart decisions, you'll need to have the right people in your corner advising and supporting you. It takes a team of experts to get the job done successfully. Whatever it is you do for your day job, presumably you do it very well. The person you hire to coordinate the sale of your home must be able to handle all aspects of the sale process as well as or better than you do your own job.

In most cases, your realtor will function as the quarterback of your home selling team. In some states you may need to hire a real estate attorney. Chances are, you may also need a stager. Perhaps you're going to need a handyman or some type of contractor to get your home ready. You may need painters, plumbers, electricians, carpet layers, and/ or landscapers. There are many vendors that may be called upon to make sure your home is in top form to extract every penny you can get for it. A great real estate agent will help you get the professionals you need in place. So, hiring the right real estate agent, who you feel will be with you every step of the way and guide your team to victory is of the utmost importance.

intuitive

How do you make sure that you hire someone that you can trust? One that makes you feel like you're on the same team and has the same objective? Most people interview two to three realtors.

- The most important thing to think about when hiring a real estate agent is to decide if the realtor has taken an appropriate amount of time to understand fully YOUR goals and YOUR particular issues and concerns. Every person who is selling a home has a unique set of reasons for doing so, and a unique set of twists and turns they will need to make to ensure a smooth and successful transition from this home to the next. Would you let a cardiac surgeon perform open-heart surgery on you without doing a full evaluation of all of your health needs? Of course not. And you shouldn't sign a listing contract with a realtor unless he or she has taken the time to fully understand your big picture and why you are doing this in the first place.

- Make sure your real estate agent is committed to real estate full-time and that it isn't a hobby or occasional endeavor. You want and need a professional.

- Get references and ask for the agent's sales history — how many homes have they sold? Does he/she have experience with homes like yours? Don't be shy about asking for performance metrics — how long do the agent's homes typically stay on the market before selling? What percent of list price do the homes ultimately sell for?

- And there is one piece of advice you should remember: please do not hire the realtor who quotes you the highest price for your home during the listing appointment. This is the worst basis upon which to make such an important hiring decision for the reasons I've covered earlier in this book.

driven

Often, the price that you actually list your home may be different than the price you think it will sell for. You need to look at a listing price as a pricing strategy. You and your realtor need to be on the same page. You need to be able to look at market data together and come up with similar, well-informed interpretations of that data. Once that's done, you're ready to hire a real estate agent. Make sure that the rest of the team of professionals this realtor works with on a daily basis will be made available to you and will treat your home and your transaction like a priority.

Once you have a team in place, it's time to delegate. You need to trust that this team knows what it's doing and will guide you to make wise decisions. Only hire someone that you trust enough to challenge your assumptions.

You may need to take their guidance at some point during the process, even if it differs from yours.

Ultimately, you should hire a team you feel confident you can trust. It's the best way to ensure you achieve the optimal result in selling your home: for the highest price, in the least amount of time, and as smoothly as possible.

well-connected

Insider Secret Revealed

Some things never change. Old-fashioned networking and making connections is still as important as ever. Since most people who will be coming to look at your home will be working with a real estate agent, a buyer's agent will play an important role in persuading or dissuading your buyer about the merits or demerits of your home. I'll let you in on an insider secret that almost no one in my industry ever discusses. If the agent you hire to list your home isn't well-liked, there may be some, and possibly many, agents who may gently guide their clients in a different direction, rather than be forced to do business with a particular agent. My fellow real estate agents are human, and just like everyone else, if they aren't acutely self-aware, they can let their own emotions go unchecked and make enemies along the way. If an agent isn't careful, a deal that went south a year ago, can cost them future deals if they didn't take care to protect their own relationships within their industry. It is imperative that effective real estate agents go to great lengths to add value to their industry, their community and their peers, to ensure that other realtors enjoy doing business with them. If they don't do this, it comes at a price to anyone who hires them to sell their home.

I firmly believe that effective real estate agents need to be emotionally invested in their communities and to work fiercely to protect the home values of their towns and their clients. This comes from donating financial resources and also donating time, rolling up their sleeves and getting involved. With these activities come deep connections of good people who have like-minded friends from other areas who want to move to your hometown. Those are the connections that are powerful for your real estate agent to be cultivating.

optimistic

SUCCESSFULLY NEGOTIATE THE SALE PRICE

We've established that selling a home can be an emotionally charged process. Emotions are heightened as a seller's home becomes a public commodity and those nosy neighbors invade once private spaces. If the home is priced correctly, some legitimate buyers will pop-up and make an offer.

By the time a seller gets to the point at which a contract is being negotiated, they're typically not in their best emotional space. Unfortunately, this is when they need to be at their emotional best. This is the moment they've been waiting for — a contract to purchase their property. Now they need to be in the right frame of mind to negotiate. When people let their emotions get in the way at this point, it can become costly in a hurry.

One thing I have learned during my real estate career is that the old adage, "The first offer is the best offer" is often true. Now, I know many people don't trust their realtors, and you may think that a realtor is simply saying the first offer is the best offer because, after all, they're probably eager to sell your home and get paid. Let me help you understand why, other than your real estate agent's eagerness to sell your home, the first offer is very often the best.

reliable

If you think about it, the best offer is most likely going to come from the person who is the most motivated to buy your home. They are going to be the one looking at the Internet every single day, in many cases multiple times a day, for homes that interest them. They are going to be the first to jump when a home that's interesting and appropriate for them comes on the market. The person that's the most motivated to buy your home, potentially the most motivated to pay the highest price, is likely not going to sit around for a month, thinking maybe they'll come, and maybe they won't. A motivated buyer will likely have transitions going on in their own life that dictate the need to buy a home quickly. Please do yourself a favor, and take that first offer very seriously. Even if it's not the price you Want, the price that feeds your Ego, the price you think you Need, or the price that incorporates what you Spent on the home. Please understand that this is likely someone who is very motivated to purchase your home.

Now, if you've looked at market information adequately, and you feel comfortable with your pricing, it's important for you to know what homes usually sell for in your area, in relation to the list price. At the time this book was written, in some of the towns that my team and I work in most often, we find that most homes sell between 95% and 98% of their list price.

honorable

Wherever you are, wherever you live, you need to know, going into this home-selling process, what that percentage is, so that you know, when you get an offer, what it is you're shooting for. If you get an offer that's 10% below asking, you should try to negotiate upward to approach that 95%-97% range, if that's what the range is in your area. If you get an offer that's 10% below your asking price, and your cool head does not prevail, you may be insulted or aggravated and not even want to deal with negotiating with that buyer. In almost every case, letting your emotions get in the way of negotiating on your first offer is almost always a bad strategy.

In addition to negotiating a contract price, there is a lot of other negotiating to be done. In most cases, you're going to be negotiating a closing date, you're going to be negotiating terms, how much cash someone will pay, how much of a deposit the buyer will put down. Will the deposits be held by real estate companies, a buyer's attorney, or a seller's attorney? What kind of inspections will be allowed on the house, as well as, what the outcome of those inspections will be? What home modifications will the buyer ask the seller to make in order to complete the transaction?

Most people who've lived in a home and feel quite comfortable there and feel they've kept their home in good condition are quite offended by getting a list of 15-20 things that need to be repaired in order for the purchaser to complete the sale. Again, anger can set in, along with frustration and many other emotions that can cloud a seller's judgment. Anticipate and embrace those emotions so that you don't let them get in the way of sound decision-making. Take some time before responding to think things through. Remind yourself what it is you're trying to accomplish. In most cases, that means selling your home for a reason that you've thought about for quite some time. Do not let your emotions get in the way of reaching that goal.

meticulous

NAVIGATE POTENTIAL LANDMINES

You now understand that emotions can get in the way of sound financial decisions. It is also important to understand what other landmines might be lurking down the line in the home selling process. Knowing which landmines might pop up allows sellers to navigate around them with the help of their trusted realtor and home selling team. If the landmine happens to explode, sellers are better positioned to handle the emotional strain without causing the transaction to fall apart. After all, the ultimate goal is to keep the transaction on track so that sellers can move on to their next destination.

The most significant and common landmine that derails transactions is the dreaded inspection. No matter how well you may have taken care of your home, the inspection report will be long and the inspector will certainly find many things to write about. Why is this the case? Inspectors are independent but they are hired by your buyers. An inspector is motivated to protect his or her own legal interests. They don't want buyers coming back and accusing them of missing an important, costly, or even dangerous safety issue. As a result, they are going to dissect your home and report everything that could potentially be wrong with your home.

masterful

Buyers, especially those that are nervous about the purchase, read the report very closely and use it as an opportunity to renegotiate the terms of the deal. This is a huge powder keg that frequently blows up! Anticipate that. Know that the inspection report will be used as ammunition to renegotiate the terms of your deal, and stay calm. It's normal to hit a roadblock at this point. Let your realtor and, in some cases, your attorney guide you through this landmine with an objective perspective. In most cases, inspection issues can be resolved with compromises and negotiated terms that are mutually acceptable to the buyer and the seller.

The second biggest landmine that causes a lot of anxiety for sellers as they head to the closing table is the buyer's mortgage financing. You've likely been told that the buyer of your home can secure a mortgage.

Just remember, there are a lot of things that can go wrong at this point. You may need to be patient to get the deal done. I've seen mortgages fall apart for a variety of reasons. For example, a buyer lost a job during the buying process and is no longer qualified for a mortgage.

POTENTIAL LANDMINES: INSPECTIONS, MORTGAGES & APPRAISALS.

creative

I've had situations where someone bought a new car while they were waiting to purchase a home, and that changed their mortgage-ability. I've experienced many, many transactions in which the buyer may qualify for a mortgage, but the bank did not feel that the home appraised at a high enough price to make it worthy of the contract.

Markets go up, markets go down, and mortgage climates change. Appraisals are something that a realtor should be able to help guide you on so you know whether or not there is likely going to be a problem. If you feel you got a terrific price for your home, don't celebrate until it appraises at or near that price. You might run into some appraisal issues. In some cases, you can negotiate this issue upfront when putting the house under contract, so that the sale is not contingent on the appraisal. Or, if you have concerns about the appraisal value of your home, it may help to have an independent appraisal completed on your home before you list it for sale.

Buyer's remorse is another landmine that you should expect.

resourceful

People get excited when they put in an offer. Sometimes they have to compete against other buyers. In some cases, they wake up the day after and say, "Oh my goodness, what have I done? I'm deathly afraid of spending $700,000 on this house or any house." I see this more often than you might expect. It can be a stumbling block but the right buyer's agent and your realtor can usually manage through this and keep the transaction on track.

Sometimes, the landmine isn't from the buyer's side. It comes from the seller. Once your home is under contract, you're probably going to shift a lot of your focus to finding your new home. This may or may not be difficult, but it's often when serious anxiety sets in. The reality of needing to leave your home and the uncertainty of where you will live can be a challenge to work through. Your realtor is a great resource, so don't be shy about expressing your concerns. Your real estate agent can ease the process and keep you on track.

Another common landmine is a gap in closing dates. The date your buyers need or want to be in your house may well be different than when you're able to get in the house that you're purchasing. This becomes a huge source of anxiety. Sometimes, the solution may mean a temporary rental, or other temporary housing, or moving twice.

sincere

That rarely makes people happy, and it's helpful to anticipate that this might be yet one more challenge you and your realtor are going to have to work through.

Lastly, I want to address delays at closing. I would say more than half of the time, houses do not close on exactly the date that is expected. Know this ahead of time so that when you are planning for your next step, you can anticipate the possibility of a delay. Have contingency plans in place so you don't find yourself homeless for a day or two.

There are myriad other issues associated with a move: finding reliable movers, items that you agreed to take care of in response to inspection requests, things breaking while moving, emotions of children leaving friends and school, your own emotions about leaving friends, and many more. Often, sellers are making life changes, as I've already outlined. There are a lot of emotional landmines that come up once your house is under contract, and the move becomes even that much more real. Again, this is normal. You're not the only person to go through the emotional rollercoaster of selling a home. Hopefully, by knowing what to anticipate and having the right team in place, you will feel a little more in control of the process and better prepared to deal with the expected and unexpected issues that may come up.

integrity

DON'T GIVE IT AWAY!

In conclusion, if you've made it all the way through this book, no doubt you've found that many of these issues ring true with you. The most important thing to remember is that when you know what to expect about the home selling process and the potential emotional and financial pitfalls that lie ahead, you are likely to feel much more in control and much less anxious about selling your home. And, more importantly, you'll avoid the costly mistakes sellers make when they let their emotions rule their decisions.

My number one goal in writing this book was to help you, as the seller, get those emotional reactions in check, so that ultimately you get the most money for your home and you Don't Give It Away!

To Your Success!

Shannon Aronson

philanthropic

SHANNON ARONSON, MSW, REALTOR

Whether guiding clients through the demanding process of selling or purchasing a home or leading fellow volunteers in meeting philanthropic goals, realtor Shannon Aronson is dedicated to serving with a purpose. Aronson's drive to help people in the many demanding stages of their lives has yielded tremendous success in her career path: first as a family therapist and now as a realtor and non-profit leader. It is her belief that service to others and financial success are synergistic elements of the modern entrepreneur.

After 7 years as a therapist, Aronson entered professional real estate as an investor and home flipper in 2002, where she demonstrated an acute understanding of where to find value in the market. Her career as a successful investor and keen understanding of the NYC suburban landscape led her down the path to becoming a realtor at Keller Williams, the international real estate franchise and #1 real estate company in the U.S. There, she has also found meaningful work with KW Cares, the charitable arm of the business.

Aronson and her team realize that for most clients, buying and selling a home is a very stressful life transition often coupled with other major changes like moving to a new community, starting a new job, or going through life-stage transitions. Understanding her clients' personalities and how their circumstances affect their decisions with regards to sales or purchases allows Shannon to tailor her strategies to each client. The end result? Concierge level service from the entire Shannon Aronson team that is designed to minimize stress during the buying and selling process. Helping clients protect their homes' value and obtaining the highest possible selling price are of paramount importance.

bold

Outside of the office, Aronson applies the same dedication to non-profit organizations such as Solstice 620, an organization she founded with her husband. Its mission is to create sustainable improvement to the lives of people in need by connecting them with professionals who are eager to donate their expertise towards helping others. She is currently Board of Trustees chair of The Education Foundation of Millburn-Short Hills, an organization in her hometown that provides funding for the township's public schools. "I believe I owe it to my clients to protect their home value by making sure their school system is elevated to the highest level possible," states Aronson. Although she has been "leaning in" long before it became common parlance, Aronson looks to altruistic corporate titans such as Sheryl Sandberg, Elon Musk, and Bill Gates for inspiration as a goal-oriented leader with service always top-of-mind.

Achieving those career goals while taking time for volunteer work, Aronson is making her mark in the world of real estate. She has been one of the very select few realtors earning the New Jersey Association of Realtors Circle of Excellence Platinum Award every year since 2011. This is the highest level obtainable within this prestigious commendation. Aronson and her team have consistently been among the very top producers in New Jersey, having been in the top 1% every year since 2009. When compared with her local competitors, she and her team outperform average agents' rankings in virtually every major category including *Days On Market, Selling Price to Listing Price* ratio, and *accurate original pricing strategies*. She has also been a finalist in *New Jersey Monthly Leading Women Entrepreneurs and Business Owners* and was ranked as one of *America's Best Real Estate Agents by REAL Trends* (in partnership with Trulia and Zillow).

thankful

Originally from the Midwest, Shannon has a Master's degree in Social Work from New York University. An 18-year resident of Short Hills, Aronson's three children have gone through the Millburn Public School system. Former singer for a local, all-female rock band, "The Mood Swings," Shannon enjoys time with her family, travel, and going into Manhattan for concerts, shows, and fun.

Information on The Shannon Aronson Group can be found at www.ShannonAronson.com.

BEFORE YOU SELL YOUR HOME

The Eleven Critical Questions To Ask A Real Estate Agent Over The Phone Before Even Taking The Time To Meet In Person ...

1. Selling a home and moving is often listed as one of the most stressful events in a lifetime. What special training do you have to help support people emotionally during this difficult transition?

2. What makes you uniquely able to assess what home preparations and expenses I should undertake to maximize my home value?

3. Can you send me materials outlining what specific processes you and your team have in place to streamline the process and ensure effective results?

4. How many homes did you list last year and how many sold? Why didn't the remaining ones sell?

5. What percentage of your business is seller representation versus buyer representation?

6. Can you give me the names and contact information for 10 clients whose homes you sold last year?

7. How many homes did you sell last year?

8. What do you do to ensure that you stay ahead of the curve on the latest marketing strategies so my property will be positioned above competing homes on the Internet?

9. What is your List Price to Sell Price ratio?

10. What special training do you have in the art of negotiation?

11. Aside from just donating money, what local charities have you helped by rolling up your sleeves and donating time and elbow grease over the last year? What work did you actually do? Do you think this has an affect on the home values in the area?